My Personal
Cookbook

These creations belong to

_____

_____

_____

_____

I will never forget the smell of my mom's kitchen, there was always an open invitation at mom's table; family or friends didn't matter to her as long as she was feeding all of us. Throughout the years they nurtured the ones they love, ladling out advice, and giving comfort when needed. There was always food for those evenings when friends dropped by on short notice, hoping for some of that comfort and hospitality they've come to expect from her kitchen and our home.

Now you can create your own memories by using this wonderful book and filling it with stories and recipes of your precious times. We hope that you will keep it in your kitchen to inspire you to create that special edition.

Carol Ann Shipman

My Personal
Cookbook
by Carol Ann Shipman

hancock

house

ISBN 0-88839-569-8
Copyright © 2004 Carol Ann Shipman

Cataloging in Publication Data

Shipman, Carol Ann, 1944–
    My personal cookbook / Carol Ann Shipman.

(Nature's gourmet series)
ISBN 0-88839-569-8

    1. Cookery. 2. Blank-books. I. Title. II. Series: Shipman, Carol Ann, 1944–. Nature's gourmet series.

TX651.S54 2004   641.5   C2004-901761-6

Printed in China—JADE

Series design and production: Nando DeGirolamo

Published simultaneously in Canada and the United States by

HANCOCK HOUSE PUBLISHERS LTD.
19313 Zero Avenue, Surrey, B.C. V3S 9R9
(604) 538-1114 Fax (604) 538-2262

HANCOCK HOUSE PUBLISHERS
1431 Harrison Avenue, Blaine, WA 98230-5005
(604) 538-1114 Fax (604) 538-2262
Web Site: www.hancockhouse.com *email:* sales@hancockhouse.com

CONTENTS

TIPS
Meat, Poultry & Fish

Meat juiciness

The amount of fat marbled through the lean meat determines the cut's juiciness. When you buy Choice cuts, the lean meat should be a deep, rich red and well-marbled with fat. The outer rim of surrounding fat should be cream-colored. Good is moderately-priced beef with less fat. It's not as juicy as Choice.

Cutting chicken

Quick and easy method to cut up chicken, use a pair of scissors. I have a pair of heavy duty sharp scissors just for preparing chicken. When cutting chicken breasts for stir-fry or cooking in chunks, lay the breast out like a hand, palm down, and cut diagonally, across the "fingers" for more tender and flavor absorbing meat.

Cooking whole fish

A hinged wire grill basket is best for cooking whole fish such as salmon. Turn fish only once. (Flipping back and forth will break fish apart.) If using a marinade, allow fish to soak up flavor for at least 30 minutes. Refrigerate while soaking in marinade.

Peeling shrimp

An ice pick can make quick work of peeling and de-veining shrimp. Just run the pick down the back towards the tail – the shell and vein are gone in one easy step!

Sashimi

When slicing Tuna (Ahi) or other fish for Sashimi, freeze the fish partially and you can slice thinner without fragmenting it.

Tastes like smoked salmon

Wrap whole cleaned salmon or other fish on a bed of herbs, both top and bottom of the fish, add slices of lemon on top, wrap up like Christmas present in newspaper, tie with butcher twine, soak in cold water, put onto BBQ over low flame. Taste will be similar to smoked fish.

Meat, Poultry & Fish

Meat, Poultry & Fish TIPS

Cooking fish in the oven

When cooking a whole fish in the oven, use a clean damp dishtowel stuffed inside the cavity. This will prevent the fish from caving in during cooking.

Chicken with buttermilk

Chicken and buttermilk just go together. Marinate your chicken in buttermilk before coating and frying. The chicken will be tender, delicious and a hit with your family or guests.

Getting under your chickens skin

To fill the cavity under the skin of a chicken. Place the chicken on a board, breast side up. Pinch the skin all over the breast of the chicken repeatedly to loosen the skin from the chicken meat. Slip one hand under the skin to separate the skin from the chicken meat. Push the your filling under the skin to cover the chicken breast completely. Sew up the cavity or close by using medal skewers.

Great gravy

To give gravy and stew great color and flavor; add a few teaspoons of soy sauce.

Meatloaf and veggies

Do your kids hate vegetables but love meatloaf? Sneak them in. Grind up carrots or spinach and add them to the meatloaf. The veggies help keep the loaf moist and the kids will never know what they are eating.

Skewers

It's either skewering, or shish kebabing, or putting that wonderful food onto the end of a green willow switch (skin the bark off first). Soak those wooden or bamboo skewers, so they don't burn. You can purchase metal ones but they do get hot.

Skewering sausage

A neat trick from the sausage world out there! Thread as many sausages onto each meat skewer as you can. Start cooking and when the time comes to turn them over, one flip turns them all.

TIPS

Meat, Poultry & Fish

The cooking pouch

A cooking "pouch" made from aluminum foil is the secret of flavorful pork chops. With this method of cooking, clean up is a breeze. Just use double sheets of foil, making these pouch any size you wish. Long and narrow, wide and fat. Play with the size. Tear off two sheets of foil. Lay them on the counter, now fold over on three sides. Now fold over again to make a good seal on all three sides. At this stage you can take some egg white and run it around the seams, this will make it seal like a rock. Fill the pouch with all kind of different things, from ribs to vegetarian dishes. Place on your BBQ or in your oven on medium to low heat. Cook to desired doneness. Look Mom No Dishes!

Carving

Proper carving insures more tender meat because slicing correctly across the grain naturally makes the individual servings easier to cut and eat. It also has economical advantages because well-carved meat and poultry yields more servings. Meat should be allowed to "repose" after it is removed from the oven in order to "firm up," thus making carving easier. Let a rare rib roast remain loosely covered in an open oven or other warm place for 20 to 30 minutes before carving. For a medium or well-done roast, about 15 minutes is adequate.

Gravy

There is only one way to make perfect gravy. Mix cold water with flour (only) to a smooth paste. Whisk briskly. Use the drippings from your meat, but make sure all the grease is removed. There are several tricks to taking off grease from your roaster some use bread slices skimmed over the top and the grease will be removed that way. Others will skim it use a grease separator. Or just spoon it off. Add your favorite gravy browning, and there you have it. Perfection!

Hot dogs

Wrap a hot dog in plastic and put it in a "Thermos" of hot water, in their lunch pail or for that special family picnic. Pack the bun separate with all there favorite condiments and guess what Mom no more soggy buns!

Cooking liver

Liver will be especially tender if first soaked in milk. Refrigerate meat a couple of hours, remove, and dry thoroughly. Bread liver if desired, then sauté until desired doneness.

Tenderize a pot roast

Tenderize a tough piece of pot roast with tomatoes. Add the tomatoes, fresh or canned, to the usual vegetables and seasonings with which you cook the meat. The acid in the tomatoes helps break down the tough fibers of the meat.

Curry powder rub

Rub chicken, pork or lamb with curry powder before roasting. Use anywhere from one to two teaspoons, depending on the size of the roast and whether you want a pronounced curry flavor or a subtle, but delicious, taste.

Stewing or braising

When you are stewing or braising, place a piece of waxed paper between the saucepan or Dutch oven and its cover. This prevents the condensation of moisture from dripping and diluting the gravy.

Grating horseradish

For tearless grated horseradish, try this: partially freeze the scraped horseradish root before you grate it. You won't shed any tears over the job.

Tenderize a steak

To tenderize a steak, brush it on both sides with a little lime juice a few hours before the steak is cooked.

TIPS

Baking and Pastry

Dotting pie with butter

To dot casserole or pie with butter, use a coarse grater to shred 'cold' butter over the dish. It's quick and effective.

Fast-rising bread dough

For faster-rising bread dough, put the bowl of dough on top of a heating pad set on low or medium. Cover with a thin cloth. Dough rises twice as fast this way.

Cutting a meringue pie

Butter your knife before cutting a meringue pie, you'll get a clean cut without damaging the meringue.

Soggy pie crust

To prevent your pumpkin or custard pie from getting a soggy crust, brush the unbaked crust with egg white then bake just a few minutes to dry the egg white and seal the crust. Add your filling and bake as usual.

Kneading bread

Knead bread dough in a large rescalable bag. Your Hands, and the counter tops, stay nice and clean.

Quick tart shells

Fit pastry over inverted muffin pans to make tart shells quickly and easily

Keeping pies juicy

One-way to protect those precious juices in a pie is with muslin or paper tape around the outside rim of the pie plate.

Keeping ladyfingers upright

To keep ladyfingers upright when they are used as a dessert shell, lightly butter the sides of the mold o spring form that is to be lined with the ladyfingers. The butter will hold them in place until you pour in the filling.

Pastry bag alternative

If pastry bag is needed and you haven't purchased any, use plastic bag, put your mixture into bag, squeeze up tight cone shape. Cut one corner of the bag, now your ready to decorate. With this method you will never have to clean a pastry bag again.

Cutting desserts

Run your knife over an open flame, such as a candle or gas stove to ensure a clean cut for cheesecakes or other desserts, where it might stick or drag while cutting dessert portions.

Keeping marshmallows

To revive marshmallows that have become hard, place them in a plastic bag with a couple slices of fresh bread. Seal the bag and after a few days the marshmallows will be as good as new.

Ground nuts

If you're making a recipe that calls for ground nuts, grinding them with a little sugar from the recipe will keep them from becoming too sticky and oily.

Greasing pans

If you are using butter for the purpose of greasing pans, be sure to use unsalted butter or you run the risk of food sticking.

Storing brown sugar

Storing brown sugar in the freezer will keep it soft.

Shelling pecans

When shelling pecans, if you want them to come out whole, pour some boiling water over the pecans and let them sit for thirty minutes before cracking.

French toast

For crispy French toast, add a touch of cornstarch to the egg mixture.

TIPS

Baking and Pastry

Chopping nuts

Before chopping nuts in a food processor, dust them with flour. This keeps the nuts from sticking to the processor.

Measuring nuts

If the recipe calls for 1 cup of nuts, chopped, then you measure whole nuts and then chop. If it says 1 cup chopped nuts, chop then measure.

Making cookie dough

Whenever I make cookie dough, I double or triple the recipe and bake only what I need at that time. I load the remaining mix into 7 ounce paper cups, placing these cups into a zip-lock bag to freeze for future baking. One 7-ounce cup holds enough dough for about a dozen freshly baked cookies. This way there is no mess to clean up and freshly baked cookies whenever you want them!

Flour duster

Keep a cheese shaker filled with flour in your baking area. When it's time to grease the pan before baking a cake, just shake some flour into the pre-greased pan.

Cake removal method

To get your cake to come out of the pan after baking line it with parchment paper before pouring the batter in. After the cake has cooled, simply turn the pan over and the cake is out – no breaking or splitting!

Moist cake mix

A tablespoon of salad oil added to your cake mix will keep the mix moist and less crumbly.

Testing a cake

If toothpicks are too short to test a cake for "doneness," a piece of uncooked spaghetti does the job.

TIPS

Baking powder

In double acting baking powder, carbon dioxide is produced when moisture is added, and again when it is heated. Using too much baking powder will produce a product with a coarse grain, and broken cell walls in the 'air' bubbles, which will cause the product to eventually fall. When you use too little, the product will not rise enough and will be heavy. Baking powders lose strength over time. They should be kept tightly covered, moisture will cause them to deteriorate faster.

If you increase the eggs in a recipe, decrease the baking powder by 1/2 teaspoon for each extra egg added, and vice versa.

French fries

Don't overfill the fry basket. This lowers the oil temperature quickly, and will produce limp fries and they will tend to stick together.

Follow directions – cook the fries at the recommended temperature for the recommended time. Old oil, dirty oil or oil that is too hot will produce fries that will not be an appetizing golden brown. Limp fries also result from too low a temperature, undercooking, and salting too soon. Wait a minute or so after they are cooked before salting them.

Whipped cream substitute

To make a whipped cream substitute in an emergency: Dissolve 1/2 cup Nonfat Dry Milk in 1/3 cup cold water. Chill Well. Whip to soft peaks. Add 1 tbsp. Lemon Juice. Whip to soft peaks again. Beat in lightly 2–4 tbsp. sugar.

Glassful

This is an old measure of volume in recipes (especially in Creole recipes) and refers to a shot glass, about 1/4 cup.

TIPS

Storing roots

Here is an old Chinese trick: fill a small clay pot (that has a lid) with plain white sand. Store fresh ginger root or ginger by burying it in the sand. It will keep for months! Much better than those dried up roots you find on your refrigerator shelves.

Decorative ice cubes

Did you get any chocolates for Christmas, Valentine's Day or Easter? Save the plastic inserts from the box and use to make decorative ice cubes for summer drinks. They can be reused many times.

Powder puff flour duster

A great flour duster is a powder puff; it's excellent for dusting pastry pans, rolling pins and working counters.

Mouse pad hot plate

Used computer mouse pads make great hot pads to protect those hot dishes from damaging your table.

A man's apron

For those macho men cooks out there, if you are not comfortable waltzing around the kitchen in those flowered aprons, buy yourself a carpenter's apron. Works great and think of what you can stuff in all those compartments.

Slicing a layer in half

To get an even cut when you want to slice a layer in two, use plain dental floss. Cut off a length, wrap it around the cake layer, cross over the ends and pull crossways so that it cuts nearly in half.

Piano wire cutter

Piano wire is a staple in my kitchen; I use it to cut cakes, pasta, cinnamon bun dough. Try it, works wonders for a lot of those baking chores.

Mixing bowl

To keep a mixing bowl still while you stir or beat in it, place the bowl on a wet, folded kitchen towel.

When cooking pasta or rice, brown long grain or wild rice, cook extra. Freeze 1-cup servings in zip lock bags. It heats quickly in the microwave for quick meals.

Cooking pasta or rice

Having a hard time peeling hard-boiled eggs? When they are finished cooling, drain them and then shake the pot vigorously so shells crack really well, then cool them in cold water. The shells practically fall off.

Peeling hard boiled eggs

Placing sugar cubes in cheese containers helps keep cheese mold-free.

Mold-free cheese

Unless the recipe calls for a specific size of egg, assume that all eggs called for are grade A large.

Egg sizes

Try pressing the whole garlic unpeeled. Remove the husk and see if this doesn't make cleaning that old stand by a lot easier.

Cleaning a garlic press

Dry roast whole, unpeeled garlic cloves in a sauté pan over medium heat for about 2 minutes or so. This will make the skins very brittle and easy to break off and discard. This will add a slightly smokey taste to the garlic which is subtle and wonderful.

Dry roast garlic

TIPS

Pesto ice cubes

Pesto ice cubes are a staple in my house. Fill ice cube trays with fresh pesto sauce and freeze it in ice cubes trays. It's then easy to use on pasta or, mixed with white wine and lemon juice, as a sauce for chicken. Sounds odd, but you can also use these pesto ice cubes in Bloody Mary's It's fabulous. Everyone should try it.

Hollandaise sauce

Commercial envelopes of hollandaise sauce frequently yield too large a quantity for just a couple of eggs benedict, or too much for a small amount of vegetables. Empty the contents of the envelope into a jar. When your ready to use the sauce mixture, melt a couple of tablespoons of butter in the microwave on low, add a equal amount of hollandaise mixture and whisk in a double amount of very cold water. Return it to the microwave, slowly heating the mixture, stop at intervals to whisk briskly. Hollandaise sauce will be ready in about 2–3 minutes.

Removing odor from your hands

To remove the odor from your hands after slicing foods such as onions or garlic, just hold a spoon between your hands and run cold water over them It's amazing, it really works!

Peeling garlic

Peel garlic by hitting it with the flat side of your knife, the peel will loosen itself off the clove. A little bit of salt sprinkled onto the clove before crushing will absorb any garlic juice that escapes.

Spice containers

Old brown Pharmacy bottles are ideal containers t use for your spices. They are dark brown in color and they have a wide mouth opening. They can still be purchased from your pharmacy or they wil direct you a source. Keeping your spices in a dark place will preserve the life span of your herbs.

Cleaning coffee pots

Clean coffee pots with ice cubes, lemon wedges and a handful of salt. Swish this mixture around for about five minutes and then wash in your dishwasher or in hot soapy water, then rinse with hot water. Clean as a whistle.

Cleaning copper pots and pans

To keep your copper shiny, scrub it with sea salt and lemon halves (nothing else). Wet the surface lightly, sprinkle a liberal amount of sea salt on the pan, cut a lemon in half, and scrub the sea salt around with the lemon half. Works better than any commercial cleanser you can buy and no possibility of chemical residue in your food.

Lighter pancakes

For a lighter pancake, replace liquid with club soda. Store only in the freezer if you have any leftovers.

Removing spices from stews and sauces

Quick and easy way to remove bay leaves or any other spice that you wish only to flavor stews and sauces with, but would like to remove before serving. Place in a tea ball. Best to use fresh whole spices, if you are using a slow cooking method. Whole herbs take longer to release their flavor.

Crystallized honey

If honey becomes crystallized, it is still good, just warm it up in a microwave or put in a pan of boiling water for a few minutes. A quick stir and it will be as good as new.

Whipped butter

Whipped butter is great, swirled into an appropriate sauce, add it, bit by bit, as you do regular butter, but because the whipped butter tastes richer, you'll find that you can get away with less.

TIPS

Protecting your cookbook

Protect your favorite cookbook; with a piece of Plexi-glass cut 12 inches by 12 inches. Place cookbook on a clean surface or cloth, open to the desired recipe and set the glass over the book.

Cleaning stainless steel

If you need to remove water spots from a stainless surface for a photo shoot or just because you are a perfectionist, you can remove them by dampening a lint-free towel with distilled vinegar or rubbing alcohol.

Hot peppers

Wear rubber gloves or surgical gloves when cleaning and preparing hot peppers.

Cooling soup in a hurry

If you need to cool a soup and you're running out of time, fill a zip lock bag with ice and slid it into the soup or cool directly over a bowl of ice.

Spraying oil on your food

A small plant water spray bottle works well for spraying oil over food. You can also purchase a perfume mist bottle. This keeps the oil delicate and helps me control the amount of oil I want to use on a salad or other dish.

Keeping food warm

Keep foods warm with rock salt the same way you use crushed ice to chill. Heat salt in pan on grill or in the oven; then put appetizers, hot potato salad, barbecue sauce in a small bowl nestled in larger pan or bowl filled with the heat salt. Keep foods warm 1 to 2 hours.

Beurre manie

Beurre manie is french for 'kneaded butter'. Equal parts of softened butter and flour, used to adjust the thickness of sauces and soups.

Non-stick pan

Ever marveled at how professional chefs' frying in omelet pans are non-stick and yours burn and catch like crazy? Well wonder no more, below is the method that will keep your pans non-stick.

1   Wash pan in warm soapy water.

2   Use a scouring pad to remove all manufacturing residue; this will also rough up surface and prepare it for seasoning.

3   Fill pan with salt and leave on a gas flame for at least 1–5 hours medium flame without disturbing.

4   Remove pan from heat (handle will be extremely hot) and empty salt into sink. It will be of extreme temperature, so do not empty into a plastic bin or bin liner.

5   Remove any residual salt by rubbing pan with paper towels (remember pan will be red hot!!).

6   Half fill pan with cooking oil (use one with a high flash point (Example Soya oil and continue on low heat for 30 minutes).

7   Remove from heat and discard the oil.

8   Remove any residual dirty oil with paper towels.

9   Rub or wipe with fresh oil before storage.

After repeated use pan will turn black; this is a sign of a durable, natural non-stick surface. Repeat steps 3 to 9 at regular intervals.

Cleaning mussels

Scrub mussels with a plastic pad. Nothing else can do as good a job removing the mess that adheres to the shells.

LIKE THIS

INGREDIENTS

1 CUP - BROWN SUGAR
1/2 CUP - MARGARINE
1 EGG.
1/4 CUP - BUTTERMILK
1 TSP. OLD FASHION
    SODA EXTRACT.
1-3/4 CUPS - FLOUR
1/2 TSP. BAKING SODA
1/2 TSP - SALT

GLAZE
2 CUPS - ICING SUGAR
1/3 CUP - MARGARINE
    (SOFT)

1-1/2 TSP ROOT BEER
    EXTRACT.

2 TBSP HOT WATER,
    PREVIOUSLY BOILED

→ EXTRACT CAN BE
PURCHASED AT A WINE
AND BEER SUPPLY
SHOP. (ROYAL OR ROYAL
PIPER IS THE BEST)

METHOD

Root Beer Cookies.

COMBINE BROWN SUGAR, MARGARINE AND MIX ON HIGH SPEED UNTIL LIGHT AND FLUFFY ADD EGG AND CONTINUE TO MIX WITH HAND BLENDER OR MIXER ADD BUTTERMILK AND ROOT BEER EXTRACT. THEN ADD BAKING SODA AND SALT THEN THE FLOUR ALL AT ONCE. MIX UNTIL SMOOTH. PREHEAT OVEN TO 350°. DROP DOUGH ON UNGREASED COOKIE SHEET BY ROUNDED TABLESPOON, I USE TWO TABLESPOONS PER COOKIE. THIS WILL ALL DEPEND ON THE SIZE OF COOKIE YOU WISH TO OBTAIN. BAKE ABOUT 8-10 MINUTES. COOL SLIGHTLY AND THEN GLAZE.

Root Beer Glaze

CREAM MARGARINE UNTIL LIGHT AND FLUFFY, ADD ICING SUGAR ALL AT ONCE, THEN ADD ROOT BEER EXTRACT AND A SMALL AMOUNT OF HOT WATER, ONE TBSP. AT A TIME. THIS ICING IS THICK AND SHOULD REMAIN THAT WAY. ICE COOKIES.

METHOD

INGREDIENTS

METHOD

INGREDIENTS

INGREDIENTS

METHOD

INGREDIENTS

INGREDIENTS

METHOD

INGREDIENTS

My Personal **Cookbook**

ETHOD

INGREDIENTS

METHOD

INGREDIENTS

ETHOD

INGREDIENTS

METHOD

INGREDIENTS

My Personal **Cookbook**

METHOD

INGREDIENTS

METHOD

INGREDIENTS

METHOD

INGREDIENTS

METHOD

INGREDIENTS

METHOD

INGREDIENTS

METHOD

INGREDIENTS

METHOD

INGREDIENTS

METHOD

INGREDIENTS

METHOD

INGREDIENTS

METHOD

INGREDIENTS

My Personal **Cookbook**

METHOD

INGREDIENTS

METHOD

INGREDIENTS

ETHOD

INGREDIENTS

INGREDIENTS

METHOD

My Personal **Cookbook**

ETHOD

INGREDIENTS

METHOD

INGREDIENTS

METHOD

INGREDIENTS

METHOD

INGREDIENTS

*My Personal **Cookbook***

METHOD

INGREDIENTS

METHOD

INGREDIENTS

METHOD

INGREDIENTS

METHOD

INGREDIENTS

METHOD

INGREDIENTS

METHOD

INGREDIENTS

METHOD

INGREDIENTS

METHOD

INGREDIENTS

INGREDIENTS

METHOD

INGREDIENTS

My Personal Cookbook

INGREDIENTS

METHOD

INGREDIENTS

METHOD

INGREDIENTS

INGREDIENTS

INGREDIENTS

METHOD

INGREDIENTS

INGREDIENTS

METHOD

INGREDIENTS

INGREDIENTS

METHOD

INGREDIENTS

METHOD

INGREDIENTS

METHOD

INGREDIENTS

INGREDIENTS

METHOD

INGREDIENTS

INGREDIENTS

INGREDIENTS

METHOD

ETHOD

INGREDIENTS

METHOD

INGREDIENTS

ETHOD

INGREDIENTS

METHOD

INGREDIENTS

ETHOD

INGREDIENTS

INGREDIENTS

METHOD

INGREDIENTS

METHOD

INGREDIENTS

INGREDIENTS

_____

_____

_____

_____

_____

_____

_____

_____

_____

_____

_____

_____

_____

_____

_____

_____

_____

_____

_____

METHOD

INGREDIENTS

*My Personal **Cookbook***

INGREDIENTS

METHOD

INGREDIENTS

METHOD

INGREDIENTS

INGREDIENTS

INGREDIENTS

METHOD

INGREDIENTS

METHOD

INGREDIENTS

METHOD

INGREDIENTS

My Personal **Cookbook**

INDEX

INDEX

INDEX

INDEX